JAMMIN' JOKES

FOR KIDS

BOB PHILLIPS
& STEVE RUSSO

HARVEST HOUSE™ PUBLISHERS

EUGENE, OREGON

JAMMIN' JOKES FOR KIDS
Copyright © 2004 by Bob Phillips and Steve Russo
Published by Harvest House Publishers
Eugene, Oregon 97402

ISBN 0-7369-1290-8

Printed in the United States of America.

04 05 06 07 08 09 / BC-CF / 10 9 8 7 6 5 4 3 2 1

Did Ya' Know?

Q: In what country are eggs dyed red at Easter time for good luck?

A: Greece.

* * *

Q: Whose search for the fountain of youth brought him to Florida in 1513?

A: Juan Ponce de Léon.

* * *

Q: What do marsupials have on their bellies?

A: A pouch for their young.

* * *

Just like fingerprints, no two lip prints are alike.

* * *

The midwestern United States has more tornadoes per year than any other area in the world.

* * *

Q: Which is bigger: Arkansas or Hungary?
A: Arkansas.

Lois & Lola

Lois: Why did the firefly keep bumping into things?

Lola: I give up.

Lois: Because he wasn't very bright.

* * *

Lois: Why did the woman wear her roller skates in her rocking chair?

Lola: I have no idea.

Lois: She wanted to rock and roll.

* * *

Lois: Why do we go to bed?

Lola: You've got me.

Lois: Because the bed will not come to us.

* * *

Lois: Why did the teacher's watch go tick, tick, tick?
Lola: I don't have the foggiest.
Lois: Because it wouldn't tock (talk) in class!

* * *

Lois: Why was the weirdo banging his head on the piano?
Lola: It's unknown to me.
Lois: He was playing by ear.

* * *

Lois: Why did the Panda get cold?
Lola: I'm in the dark.
Lois: Because he slept in his bear skin.

* * *

Lois: Why did the tree try to get sunburned?
Lola: Search me.
Lois: He wanted to be a redwood.

* * *

Lois: Why was the little piece of ice like his dad?
Lola: I have no clue.
Lois: Because he was a chip off the cold block.

* * *

Lois: Why did the teacher send the clock to the principal's office?
Lola: I don't know.
Lois: For "tocking" too much.

* * *

Lois: Why is a cake like a baseball team?
Lola: Beats me.
Lois: Both need a good batter.

Did Ya' Know?

Slugs have four noses.

* * *

Polar bears can live for almost six months without eating.

* * *

The eyes of the giant squid are 15 inches across—larger than the eyes of any other animal.

* * *

The average person spends more than 20 years of his or her life sleeping.

* * *

Q: How long does it take a plucked eyebrow to grow back?

A: About 92 days.

* * *

There are 86,400 seconds in a day.

Clayton & Clementine

Clayton: What would you be doing if you washed a pound of clothes a day for two thousand days?

Clementine: I have no clue.

Clayton: Washington.

$$* \quad * \quad *$$

Clayton: What do you get when you cross a steer with a tadpole?

Clementine: I don't know.

Clayton: A bullfrog.

$$* \quad * \quad *$$

Clayton: What's a shark's favorite book?

Clementine: Beats me.

Clayton: Huckleberry Finn.

$$* \quad * \quad *$$

Clayton: What kind of horses go out at night?

Clementine: I can't guess.

Clayton: Night mares!

* * *

Clayton: What two letters describe a box with nothing in it?

Clementine: I have no idea.

Clayton: M T (em-tee).

* * *

Clayton: What do they call a man who eats elephants?

Clementine: You tell me.

Clayton: Big mouth.

* * *

Clayton: What do you call a kangaroo that's too lazy to leave its mother's pouch?

Clementine: I give up.

Clayton: A pouch potato.

* * *

Clayton: What happens when you don't dust your mirror?

Clementine: Who knows?

Clayton: It gives you a dirty look.

* * *

Clayton: What telephone company do Olympics runners use?

Clementine: You've got me.

Clayton: Sprint.

Did Ya' Know?

Q: Before 1600, Europeans had no sugar. What did they sweeten their cookies with?

A: Honey. They called them "honey cakes."

* * *

Q: The letter *e* is the most commonly used letter in English. What's the next most common letter?

A: It's *t*.

* * *

Our tongues have 20,000 highly sensitive taste buds.

* * *

Coconuts can sometimes travel thousands of miles. They fall off trees next to beaches, land in the ocean water, then float up onto faraway beaches and sprout into new trees.

* * *

Q: How much does a baby robin eat?

A: Fourteen feet of earthworms every day.

* * *

Q: Gingerbread cookies are associated with what holiday?

A: Christmas. They are used for decoration as well as a treat.

Abbot & Abner

Abbot: Why is Cinderella such a bad baseball player?
Abner: I have no clue.
Abbot: Because she had a pumpkin for a coach.

* * *

Abbot: What do your teacher and parents have in common?
Abner: I don't know.
Abbot: They both give you homework.

* * *

Abbot: What do you call a spelling bee in Alaska?
Abner: Beats me.
Abbot: A cold spell.

* * *

Abbot: What do mice use to keep their drinks cold?
Abner: I can't guess.
Abbot: Mice cubes.

* * *

Abbot: What do you call a rock with eight legs?
Abner: I have no idea.
Abbot: A rocktopus.

* * *

Abbot: What do you call a hen that is jealous?
Abner: You tell me.
Abbot: Hen-vious.

* * *

Abbot: What do you call a polar bear in the Caribbean?
Abner: I give up.
Abbot: Lost.

* * *

Abbot: What travels all around the world but stays in one corner?

Abner: Who knows?

Abbot: A postage stamp.

* * *

Abbot: What did the violin maker say when he made a mistake?

Abner: You've got me.

Abbot: "Oh, fiddlesticks!"

* * *

Abbot: What is an astronaut's favorite food?

Abner: My mind is blank.

Abbot: Moon pie!

Did Ya' Know?

The phrase "he wears his heart on his sleeve" dates from the 1700s, when men would wear their Valentine sweetheart's name pinned to their shirt sleeve.

* * *

Q: Did you know that the heart does enough work during an hour to lift 3,000 pounds?

A: That's enough to lift an adult giraffe.

* * *

Q: What is the oldest regularly run footrace in the United States?

A: The Boston Marathon, first run in 1897.

* * *

Q: Which is bigger: Indiana or Austria?

A: Indiana.

✳ ✳ ✳

Q: In what country was the word *pants* considered dirty?

A: England, during the 1880s.

Barnabas & Bartholomew

Barnabas: What sort of chair should you sit in while sorting your stone collection?

Bartholomew: I have no clue.

Barnabas: A rocking chair.

* * *

Barnabas: What did one frog say to the other?

Bartholomew: I don't know.

Barnabas: Time sure is fun when you're having flies.

* * *

Barnabas: What do you call a person who always carries an encyclopedia in their pocket?

Bartholomew: Beats me.

Barnabas: Smarty pants.

* * *

Barnabas: What do pigs wear when they go swimming?

Bartholomew: I can't guess.

Barnabas: Hoggles.

* * *

Barnabas: What does a cow sit on?

Bartholomew: I have no idea.

Barnabas: A "cow"ch.

* * *

Barnabas: What do you call it when a lamb sneaks up on someone?

Bartholomew: You tell me.

Barnabas: A lamb bush.

* * *

Barnabas: What do you call a hen who is specially trained to design and build things?

Bartholomew: I give up.

Barnabas: A hen-gineer.

* * *

Barnabas: What is the first thing you do in the morning?

Bartholomew: Who knows?

Barnabas: You wake up.

* * *

Barnabas: What side dish do coal miners eat for lunch?

Bartholomew: You've got me.

Barnabas: Coal slaw.

* * *

Barnabas: What happened to the dog that swallowed the clock?

Bartholomew: My mind is blank.

Barnabas: He got a lot of ticks!

Did Ya' Know?

Most dogs have pink tongues except the Chow Chow. This breed has a blue tongue.

* * *

Q: How far is the earth from the sun?
A: 93 million miles (approx.).

* * *

If you drank as much water as a cow, you would have 240 glasses of water every day.

* * *

Q: How wide can a hippo open its mouth?
A: Wide enough for a four-foot tall child to fit inside.

* * *

Q: How long a line can the typical #2 pencil write until there's nothing left?

A: 35 miles.

* * *

By age 65, the average person has spent nine years watching television.

* * *

Q: Which is bigger: Iowa or Portugal?

A: Iowa.

Leftovers

Bob: I value your opinion. What do you think of the latest joke book I have written?

Ken: Frankly, it's worthless.

Bob: I know, but I'd like to hear your opinion just the same.

* * *

Christy: I heard that someone in Russia owns a talking cow. Do you know who it is?

Lisa: I think it is Ma's cow.

* * *

I don't want to say that the food in our school cafeteria is bad, but you get a prescription with every meal.

* * *

First mother: I finally got my son to stop biting his nails.

Second mother: How did you do that?

First mother: I bought him some shoes.

* * *

Melba: If a ghost had a ghost rooster, what would it say?

Pam: Cock-a-doodle-boo.

* * *

Melba: If a ghost were to make a mistake, what would you call it?

Pam: A boo-boo.

* * *

Larry: Let's have a race to see who can say the alphabet first.

Gary: Okay, I'm ready.

Larry: The alphabet.

* * *

Rich: Do you know what happened to the Italian glass-blower?

Dave: I have no idea.

Rich: He inhaled and got a pane in his stomach.

* * *

Eddie: I think it is best if you eat French fries with your fingers.

Freddie: Actually, I prefer to eat fingers separately.

* * *

Brother: Oh, I've got a splinter in my finger!

Sister: You must have been scratching your head.

Did Ya' Know?

Pain signals travel along our nerves at about 50 feet per second.

* * *

Q: How far does an office chair with casters or wheels typically roll in a year?

A: Eight miles.

* * *

The longest bicycle ever built was more than 66 feet long and seated 35 people.

* * *

About 11 percent of the world's population is left-handed.

* * *

By age 10 the average American child has worn down 730 crayons.

* * *

Q: What is the largest kind of spider?

A: The tarantula. Some South American tarantulas can grow as large as dinner plates.

Christopher & Clara

Christopher: What's always behind the times?
Clara: I have no clue.
Christopher: The back of a clock.

* * *

Christopher: What do you call a rabbit that changes tires on cars?
Clara: I don't know.
Christopher: A jackrabbit.

* * *

Christopher: What does a robot take for a bad cough?
Clara: Beats me.
Christopher: Robot-tussin.

* * *

Christopher: What do you get when you cross a hummingbird with a doorbell?

Clara: I can't guess.

Christopher: A humdinger.

* * *

Christopher: What happened when the couple tried to kiss on a foggy day?

Clara: I have no idea.

Christopher: They mist.

* * *

Christopher: What vegetable do you find in crowded stores and buses?

Clara: You tell me.

Christopher: Squash.

* * *

Christopher: What do you buy for someone who has everything?

Clara: I give up.

Christopher: A burglar alarm.

* * *

Christopher: What did Santa say when he first spotted the new world?

Clara: Who knows?

Christopher: Land ho ho ho!

* * *

Christopher: What is a pig's favorite ballet?

Clara: You've got me.

Christopher: Swine Lake.

* * *

Christopher: What's the richest kind of air?

Clara: My mind is blank.

Christopher: A millionaire.

Did Ya' Know?

It takes 548 peanuts to make a 12-ounce jar of peanut butter.

* * *

Q: What is a baby fish called?

A: Newly hatched baby fish are called *fry*. They are known to hide in their parents' mouths when they think they are in danger.

* * *

A large raindrop can fall at a speed of 22 miles per hour.

* * *

Peanuts aren't nuts; they're beans.

* * *

Q: Of the world's 193 countries, what five contain half of the world's population?

A: Brazil, China, India, Indonesia, and the United States.

* * *

Turkeys have a 300-degree range of vision because their eyes are on the sides of their head. That's almost like having eyes on the back of your head.

How Now?

Q: How long can a grown crocodile go without food?
A: Two years.

* * *

Tony: How can I find out how big my pet skunk is?
Kati: Use a scent-meter (centimeter) ruler.

* * *

Q: How do you put on a great space party?
A: Planet (plan it)!

* * *

P.K.: How do you make a banana shake?
Kelley: Take it to a scary movie.

* * *

Q: How did the rabbit make gold soup?
A: He used 24 carrots.

* * *

Q: How do you make a fruit punch?
A: Give it boxing lessons.

* * *

Q: How do angels answer the phone?
A: Halo!

* * *

Q: How do you make the word *one* disappear?
A: Put a *g* in front of it and it's *gone!*

* * *

Q: How do robins get into shape?
A: They do worm-ups!

* * *

Q: How many peas are there in a pint?
A: There is only one *p* in *pint*.

* * *

Q: How is math done on a farm?
A: With a "cow"culator.

* * *

Q: How does a caterpillar start its day?
A: It turns over a new leaf.

* * *

Q: How did the note escape from the sheet music?
A: It slipped out through the bars.

Did Ya' Know?

True or false: Your funny bone isn't actually a bone.
True. It's a nerve.

* * *

Q: What country has the greatest concentration of volcanoes?
A: Indonesia, with 140.

* * *

The largest jack-o'-lantern in the world was carved from an 827-pound pumpkin.

* * *

Seventy-five percent of the dust in your house is made up of dead skin cells.

＊ ＊ ＊

Q: What was the first state in the United States?
A: Delaware.

The Answer Man

Q: Where did the first cow in space end up?
A: The Milky Way.

* * *

Q: Who pulls teeth and loves camping?
A: The tentist.

* * *

Q: Do you know what the first elevator said to the second elevator?
A: I think I'm coming down with something.

* * *

Q: If every dog has his day, then what does a dog with a broken tail have?
A: A "weak" end.

* * *

Q: Did you hear about the crazy person who went around saying no all the time?

A: No. I think I've found him.

* * *

Q: Did you hear about the computer that caught a virus?

A: Yeah. It started out as a cough he caught from a hacker.

* * *

Q: Did you hear about the new show featuring home movies of kids without Kleenex?

A: It's called America's Runniest Nose Videos.

* * *

Did you hear about the neighbor who was so grouchy that her dog put up a sign that said "Beware of Owner"?

* * *

Q: Which two mountains are opposites?
A: Mount Everest and Mount Rushmore.

* * *

Q: Which instrument plays only sour notes?
A: The pickle-o (piccolo).

* * *

Q: Which movie features Rick Moranis as a guy who helps sea creatures lose weight?
A: *Honey, I Shrunk the Squids.*

* * *

Q: Which movie is about a lot of lobsters?
A: *101 Crustaceans.*

Did Ya' Know?

In Australia, a hurricane is called a *willy-willy*.

* * *

Q: Where can you find the most drops of fresh water on Earth?

A: About 99 out of every 100 drops of fresh water on this globe are frozen inside a cap of ice on a mountain-top or in a glacier.

* * *

People eat more bananas than any other fruit in the world.

* * *

Humans can hear 1,500 different pitches.

* * *

The world's biggest sweet potato weighed more than 40 pounds.

* * *

Q: What was the ancient Greek remedy for soothing an upset stomach?

A: Gingerbread cookies (special honey cakes).

Gus & Gabriel

Gus: What does a leg wear to keep warm?
Gabriel: I have no clue.
Gus: A kneecap.

* * *

Gus: What kind of fruit should you feed to a scarecrow?
Gabriel: I don't know.
Gus: Strawberries.

* * *

Gus: What is a sound sleeper?
Gabriel: Beats me.
Gus: Someone who snores.

* * *

Gus: What do you call a grandfather clock?
Gabriel: I can't guess.
Gus: An old-timer.

* * *

Gus: What did the pig say when he was hot?
Gabriel: I have no idea.
Gus: I'm bacon (bakin').

* * *

Gus: What word has the most letters in it?
Gabriel: You tell me.
Gus: *Mailbox.*

* * *

Gus: What kind of tree do you find in a kitchen?
Gabriel: I give up.
Gus: A pantry.

* * *

Gus: What flowers eat cookies?

Gabriel: Who knows?

Gus: Tulips (two lips).

* * *

Gus: What did one math book say to the other math book?

Gabriel: You've got me.

Gus: I have too many problems.

* * *

Gus: What do you call dinosaur auto accidents?

Gabriel: My mind is blank.

Gus: T-wrecks.

Did Ya' Know?

Q: What other creatures, besides birds, have a beak?
A: Turtles and octopuses.

* * *

The largest iceberg ever found was 208 miles long and 60 miles wide. That's bigger than Massachusetts.

* * *

Dolphins sleep with one eye open.

* * *

Each of your feet hits the ground about 7,000 times a day.

* * *

After bananas, a zoo gorilla's favorite food is celery.

Q: How much trash does each American toss out every year?

A: About 1,500 pounds—equal to the size and weight of one big cow.

Caesar & Cybil

Caesar: What do cats eat for breakfast?

Cybil: I have no clue.

Caesar: Mice Crispies.

* * *

Caesar: What do you get when you cross a turkey with a knife?

Cybil: I don't know.

Caesar: Thanksgiving dinner.

* * *

Caesar: What animal is big, white, and shaped like a tooth?

Cybil: Beats me.

Caesar: A "molar" bear.

* * *

Caesar: What did the snowman say when he got lost?
Cybil: I can't guess.
Caesar: We're in the middle of snow where.

* * *

Caesar: What do cows have on their ice cream?
Cybil: I have no idea.
Caesar: Chocolate mooooousse!

* * *

Caesar: What cookie flavor is also used in perfume?
Cybil: You tell me.
Caesar: Vanilla.

* * *

Caesar: What washes up on really small beaches?
Cybil: I give up.
Caesar: Microwaves!

* * *

Caesar: What kind of nail can't be driven into wood?
Cybil: Who knows?
Caesar: A fingernail.

* * *

Caesar: What can you hold without touching it?
Cybil: You've got me.
Caesar: A conversation.

* * *

Caesar: What do you call a big gray animal who needs a bath?
Cybil: My mind is blank.
Caesar: A smell-ephant.

Did Ya' Know?

Q: What city has the largest Polish population outside of Warsaw, Poland?

A: Chicago, Illinois.

* * *

In a year, the average American walks four miles while making his or her bed.

* * *

During the Middle Ages (from about A.D. 500 to 1500) people used spider webs to try to cure warts.

* * *

Q: What animal's eye is bigger than its brain?

A: The ostrich.

* * *

Track athletes are most likely to break records later in the day when their body temperatures are at their highest.

Open the Door

Knock, knock.
Who's there?
Waiter.
Waiter who?
Waiter minute while I tie my shoe.

* * *

Knock, knock.
Who's there?
Amanda.
Amanda who?
Amanda fix your washing machine.

* * *

Knock, knock.
Who's there?
Hominy.
Hominy who?
Hominy times do I have to knock at your door?

* * *

Knock, knock.
Who's there?
Iguana.
Iguana who?
Iguana hold your hand . . .

* * *

Knock, knock.
Who's there?
Kent.
Kent who?
Kent you just wait till I tell you another knock-knock joke?

* * *

Knock, knock.
Who's there?
Miniature.
Miniature who?
Miniature open your mouth, you may put your foot in it.

* * *

Knock, knock.
Who's there?
Caesar.
Caesar who?
Caesar jolly good fellow . . .

* * *

Knock, knock.
Who's there?
Eiffel.
Eiffel who?
Eiffel off the step and hurt my foot.

* * *

Knock, knock.
Who's there?
Stan.
Stan who?
Stan back quick; I think I'm going to be sick.

* * *

Knock, knock.
Who's there?
Razor.
Razor who?
Razor hands. This is a holdup.

* * *

Knock, knock.
Who's there?
Hiram.
Hiram who?
Hiram fine. How are you?

Did Ya' Know?

Q: Where is it easier to catch a cold—at home or in Antarctica?

A: At home. It's so chilly in Antarctica that most germs can't survive.

* * *

Q: Which is bigger: Florida or England?

A: Florida.

* * *

Your lungs contain almost 1,500 miles of airways.

* * *

The average birthweight of a gorilla is four pounds, 14 ounces.

* * *

Q: Do grasshoppers have ears?

A: Yes. One on each side of their abdomen.

* * *

Q: How does a sea otter keep warm and dry in cold water?

A: With help from its thick, fuzzy coat. Just one square inch of a sea otter's skin is covered with over 170,000 hairs. That's more than you have on your whole head.

Geraldine & Gaspar

Geraldine: Why do bears live in caves?

Gaspar: I have no clue.

Geraldine: Because they can't afford apartments in the city.

* * *

Geraldine: Why do you handle a cookie carefully?

Gaspar: I don't know.

Geraldine: Because chocolate chips.

* * *

Geraldine: Why did the cookie cry?

Gaspar: Beats me.

Geraldine: Because its mother had been a wafer (away for) so long!

* * *

Geraldine: Why don't bananas ever get lonely?

Gaspar: I can't guess.

Geraldine: Because they go around in bunches.

* * *

Geraldine: Why didn't the moon eat its dinner?

Gaspar: I have no idea.

Geraldine: Because it was full!

* * *

Geraldine: Why didn't Katie take the math test?

Gaspar: You tell me.

Geraldine: She wanted to save it for a brainy day.

* * *

Geraldine: Why did the annoying exterminator lose his job?

Gaspar: I give up.

Geraldine: He bugged his boss.

* * *

Geraldine: Why did the man put his dog in a bag?

Gaspar: Who knows?

Geraldine: It was a doggie bag.

* * *

Geraldine: Why was the baseball player invited to go camping?

Gaspar: You've got me.

Geraldine: Because they needed someone to pitch the tent.

* * *

Geraldine: Why did the cowgirl name her horse *Ink?*

Gaspar: My mind is blank.

Geraldine: Because it kept running out of the pen.

* * *

Geraldine: Why do you have a big black eye, son?

Gaspar: I dropped a baseball bat on a foot.

Geraldine: That doesn't explain the black eye.

Gaspar: Well, you see, it wasn't my foot.

Did Ya' Know?

Q: Where were chocolate chip cookies invented?

A: In Massachusetts in 1935 by Mrs. Ruth Wakefield of the Toll House Restaurant.

✳ ✳ ✳

Q: In which country were Chinese fortune cookies invented?

    A. United States   C. China
    B. Hungary   D. Japan

A: The United States. They were invented by Chinese immigrants.

✳ ✳ ✳

Q: What are the world's crumbliest cookies?

A: Shortbread cookies.

✳ ✳ ✳

Q: What is the largest cookie ever made?

A: A 40- by 50-foot oatmeal-chocolate chip cookie topped with Italian butter cream icing. It was baked on May 20, 1995.

* * *

Q: Which is bigger: Alabama or Greece?

A: Alabama.

Luann & Lowell

Luann: What do rabbits put into their computers?

Lowell: I have no clue.

Luann: Hoppy discs.

* * *

Luann: What does a chickadee say when it's very hungry?

Lowell: I don't know.

Luann: Long time, no seed.

* * *

Luann: What's the best way to see Europe in the morning?

Lowell: Beats me.

Luann: Look in the mirror and you'll see Europe (you're up)!

* * *

Luann: What's a cow's favorite fruit?
Lowell: I can't guess.
Luann: Cattleloupe.

* * *

Luann: What do you call a balanced diet?
Lowell: I have no idea.
Luann: An ice cream sandwich in each hand.

* * *

Luann: What kind of weather pleases a duck?
Lowell: You tell me.
Luann: Fowl weather.

* * *

Luann: What did the Texas farmer say to the man who wanted to buy a dachshund?
Lowell: I give up.
Luann: Go ahead, get a long little doggie.

* * *

Luann: What do you get when you put a duck and a firecracker together?

Lowell: Who knows?

Luann: A firequacker.

* * *

Luann: What is a cat's favorite dessert?

Lowell: You've got me.

Luann: Mice cream.

Did Ya' Know?

The average human brain weighs three pounds.

* * *

Q: Lincoln Logs were invented in 1916 by whom?
A: The son of architect Frank Lloyd Wright.

* * *

Q: How far across is the largest crater on the moon?
A: 183 miles.

* * *

One-third of all ice cream sold in the United States is vanilla.

* * *

Q: How much does a hummingbird weigh?

A: Less than a penny.

* * *

Q: Which is bigger: Kansas or the Netherlands?

A: Kansas.

* * *

Q: What color appears most frequently in the northern lights?

A: Pale green.

Tongue Twisters

Shy sly slim Sheriff Shultz slays seven sly shy slithering snakes.

* * *

Billy Blob's big blue blister burst.

* * *

The gray ghost goes by Barney Booth's Blue Goose bus.

* * *

The silent shark ate sheep in the cheap sheep soup shop.

* * *

Peggy Paddock peddles Ping-Pong paddles.

* * *

A capable cook cooked cupcakes in a cook's cap.

* * *

Sally safely sells seven shapely socks.

* * *

Susan shocked silly Sally with shocking shoes and socks.

Did Ya' Know?

Seals can stay under water for as long as 70 minutes without coming up for air.

* * *

Q: How many different kinds of spiders are there in the world?

A: 36,000 known kinds.

* * *

A praying mantis will attack any small form of animal life except an ant.

* * *

The average American eats 91 pounds of bacon per year.

* * *

Ten inches of snow equals one inch of water.

* * *

Q: When a skunk raises its tail, stomps its feet, and hisses, you're in for a squirt. How far can a skunk spray its stinky scent?

A: More than 10 feet.

Mix and Match

Teacher: I tried to teach you everything I know.
Student: I know, and I'm still ignorant.

* * *

Jeff: I have to go to the hospital later. What is the fastest way to get there?
Noel: Stand in the middle of the road.

* * *

Boyfriend: Honey, here are some sweets for the sweet.
Girlfriend: Thank you very much. Won't you have some of these nuts?

* * *

Jon: Well, Joe, when you get to New York, you should take a cruise of New York Harbor.

Joe: How fast does the boat go?

Jon: About 20 knots an hour.

Joe: Wow! How long does it take to untie the knots?

* * *

Juliet: O Romeo, Romeo! Wherefore art thou Romeo?

Romeo: Down here in the flowers. The trellis broke.

* * *

Melba: Swimming is one of the best exercises for keeping slim.

Pam: Did you ever see a sea lion?

* * *

Kati: Are there eggs on the menu?

Waiter: No. We clean the menus every day.

* * *

Jeff: Oh, by the way, Noel, next week I am going to New York.

Noel: Are you going to go by Buffalo?

Jeff: Don't be silly. I am going to go by train.

* * *

Gabi: Waiter! I just caught a fly.

Waiter: Great! I'll put it in tomorrow's soup.

* * *

Patient: What should I do when my ear rings?
Doctor: Answer it!

* * *

Teacher: What is the matter, Arthur?

Arthur: I'm very sick.

Teacher: Where does it hurt the most?

Arthur: At school.

Did Ya' Know?

Q: How many eyes do spiders have?

A: Some have as many as eight eyes, but they have lousy vision.

* * *

Q: What is the only place in the world where spiders do not live?

A: Antarctica.

* * *

Q: What insect generates three times more lift in proportion to weight than the most advanced man-made aircraft?

A: The dragonfly.

* * *

Q: What are comets made of?

A: Even though they look like globes of fire, they're really made of ice and dust. People used to call them "hairy stars."

* * *

Q: If the sun's core burned out today, how soon would the earth feel the effect?

A: Scientists say the solar surface would cool so slowly it would take 10 million years for earth to feel the effect.

Walrus & Willis

Walrus: What happens when the whole planet gets sunburned?

Willis: I have no clue.

Walrus: There's a massive earth flake.

* * *

Walrus: What should you do if the beach is really crowded?

Willis: I don't know.

Walrus: Get on the wading list.

* * *

Walrus: What do you get when you cross a telephone with a pair of pants?

Willis: Beats me.

Walrus: Bell bottoms.

* * *

Walrus: What's the coldest part of a cake?

Willis: I can't guess.

Walrus: The icing.

* * *

Walrus: What did the waitress say when the big wave hit the beach party?

Willis: I have no idea.

Walrus: Dinner is surfed.

* * *

Walrus: What do you call someone who sits behind a lifeguard at a pool?

Willis: You tell me.

Walrus: Backseat diver.

* * *

Walrus: What were the two talkative computers doing?

Willis: I give up.

Walrus: They were having a disc-ussion.

* * *

Walrus: What did the sock say to the shoe?
Willis: Who knows?
Walrus: You're putting me on.

* * *

Walrus: What kind of bell doesn't ring?
Willis: You've got me.
Walrus: A dumbbell.

Did Ya' Know?

Q: Which is bigger: West Virginia or Belgium?
A: West Virginia.

* * *

You blink about 10,000 times a day.

* * *

A spacecraft must reach the speed of 24,800 miles per hour before it can escape Earth's gravity.

* * *

It takes only 15 muscles to smile, but it takes 43 muscles to frown.

* * *

Q: What unique coin denomination was issued by the U.S. mint between 1851 and 1889?

A: The three-cent piece.

Agatha & Alonzo

Agatha: What did the Martians have for lunch?

Alonzo: I have no clue.

Agatha: Martian-mallows!

* * *

Agatha: What bird forgets people's names?

Alonzo : I don't know.

Agatha: An owl, because it's always saying whooo!

* * *

Agatha: What did the mother frog say when her eggs hatched?

Alonzo : Beats me.

Agatha: Hoppy (happy) birthday!

* * *

Agatha: What did the lightning bug say to his teenage son?

Alonzo : I can't guess.

Agatha: I don't want you to go out tonight.

* * *

Agatha: What did the flea say when he got tangled in the leopard's fur?

Alonzo : I have no idea.

Agatha: I'm in a tight spot.

* * *

Agatha: What magazines do dogs read?

Alonzo : You tell me.

Agatha: *Chewsweek, Digger's Digest,* and *Better Bones & Gardens.*

* * *

Agatha: What five-letter word has six left after you take two away?

Alonzo : I give up.

Agatha: The word *sixty*.

* * *

Agatha: What type of bug likes TV?

Alonzo: Who knows?

Agatha: The brown-banded cockroach loves to eat the insulation in a TV set.

* * *

Agatha: What do you call a row of bunnies walking backward?

Alonzo: You've got me.

Agatha: A receding hare line.

* * *

Agatha: What do you get when you cross a penguin with a leopard?

Alonzo: My mind is blank.

Agatha: I don't know, but it wears a polka-dot tuxedo!

Did Ya' Know?

The amount of ice cream people eat in one year could fill the Grand Canyon.

* * *

The Chihuahua Whiptail lizard flicks its tongue out of its mouth more than 700 times an hour.

* * *

Q: What is the world's fastest bird?

A: The peregrine falcon. It can swoop at speeds of over 124 miles per hour.

* * *

Q: How long is the average life span of a U.S. $1 bill?

A: 18 months.

* * *

A newborn chick will follow the first thing that moves.

* * *

Q: In which country do the people eat the most cookies in the world?

A: The Netherlands. The Dutch eat an average of 58.28 pounds of cookies per individual each year. People in the United States eat only 12 pounds of cookies per individual each year.

Bernard & Bessie

Bernard: What do you get when you cross a rooster with a giraffe?

Bessie: I have no clue.

Bernard: A wake-up alarm for people on the top floor.

* * *

Bernard: What did the cowboy say when his dog fell in the fire?

Bessie: I don't know.

Bernard: Hot dog!

* * *

Bernard: What is a rabbit's favorite jewelry?

Bessie: Beats me.

Bernard: Fourteen-carrot (karat) gold!

* * *

Bernard: What was an "owie" called in prehistoric times?

Bessie: I can't guess.

Bernard: A dino-sore (dinosaur).

* * *

Bernard: What kind of sandwich sinks to the bottom of your stomach?

Bessie: You tell me.

Bernard: A sub!

* * *

Bernard: What is a librarian's favorite food?

Bessie: I give up.

Bernard: Shhhh-kebab (shish kebab).

* * *

Bernard: What did George Washington say to his men before they crossed the Delaware?

Bessie: Who knows?

Bernard: Get in the boat!

* * *

Bernard: What has just three letters, but is not small?

Bessie: You've got me.

Bernard: Big!

* * *

Bernard: What did the egg do when it heard a funny joke?

Bessie: My mind is a blank.

Bernard: It cracked up!

Did Ya' Know?

The largest turkey in the world was raised in England in 1989. It tipped the scales at 86 pounds—about the weight of an average 12-year-old child.

***

Caterpillars have 4,000 muscles in their bodies. Humans only have 639.

***

Q: What word in the English language is used more than any other?

A: *The.*

***

Q: What percentage of the earth's land is desert?

A: Twenty-four percent.

✳ ✳ ✳

Some mantis shrimp travel by doing backward somersaults.

Winston & Wallace

Winston: What goes gobble, gobble, bang?

Wallace: I have no clue.

Winston: A turkey in a minefield.

* * *

Winston: What do they call a camel without any humps?

Wallace: I don't know.

Winston: Humphrey (hump free).

* * *

Winston: What kind of clothing does your pet cat wear?

Wallace: Beats me.

Winston: A petticoat.

* * *

Winston: What is the best thing to do for a very sick wasp?

Wallace: I can't guess.

Winston: Take it to the waspital.

* * *

Winston: What is the difference between a butcher and a light sleeper?

Wallace: I have no idea.

Winston: One weighs a steak and the other stays awake.

* * *

Winston: What would happen if you tickled the ivories?

Wallace: You tell me.

Winston: It would make the piano laugh.

* * *

Winston: What is the difference between a school-teacher and a railway engineer?

Wallace: I give up.

Winston: One minds the train and the other trains the mind.

* * *

Winston: What is doughy, covered with tomato paste, and is over 50 yards tall?

Wallace: Who knows?

Winston: The Leaning Tower of Pizza.

* * *

Winston: What do you get when you cross a hippopotamus with a kangaroo?

Wallace: You've got me.

Winston: Great big holes all over Australia.

* * *

Winston: What is worse than a centipede with sore feet?

Wallace: That's a mystery.

Winston: A giraffe with a sore throat.

Did Ya' Know?

A rattlesnake, on average, rattles its tail only two times for each year of its life.

* * *

When a puffer fish gets scared, it gulps down water and inflates like a ball. This scares its enemies and allows it to escape.

* * *

Q: How many arrows are clutched in the talon of the bald eagle on the $1 bill?

A: Thirteen—representing the 13 colonies.

* * *

Q: What do you call a newborn giraffe?

A: A calf.

* * *

The mousetrap is the "most invented" machine in American history. More than 4,400 versions have been patented.

* * *

Kangaroos can hop at speeds up to 40 miles per hour, but they cannot walk.

Alvin & Amos

Alvin: What do you get when you cross an elephant and a parrot?

Amos: I don't know.

Alvin: Something that tells everything it remembers.

* * *

Alvin: What kind of cow eats with its tail?

Amos: Beats me.

Alvin: They all do. Cows do not remove their tails when they eat.

* * *

Alvin: What is the most famous fish in Hollywood?

Amos: I can't guess.

Alvin: The starfish.

* * *

Alvin: What do you get when you dial (209) 557-3796-643-2239, extension 7956?

Amos: I have no idea.

Alvin: A blister on your finger.

* * *

Alvin: What does a baby elephant do when daddy elephant is about to sneeze?

Amos: You tell me.

Alvin: He gets out of the way fast.

* * *

Alvin: What do they call the animal that is a cross between an insect and a rabbit?

Amos: I give up.

Alvin: Bugs Bunny.

* * *

Alvin: What time is spelled forward and backward yet remains the same?

Amos: Who knows?

Alvin: Noon.

* * *

Alvin: What is the most silent tongue?

Amos: You've got me.

Alvin: The tongue in your shoe.

* * *

Alvin: What is yellow, long, and goes slam-slam-slam-slam?

Amos: My mind is blank.

Alvin: A four-door banana.

Did Ya' Know?

Every year, more than four billion flowers are sold in Holland.

* * *

The average person laughs about 540,000 times during his or her life.

* * *

Q: Besides the moon, what else orbits around the earth?

A: Thousands of pieces of space junk, such as screws, astronaut gloves, pieces from old rockets, and even paint chips. In 1983, a paint chip traveling at 8,000 miles per second smashed through a space shuttle window.

* * *

Q: How many aluminum cans are recycled each year in the United States?

A: About 40 billion.

Cyrus & Cora

Cyrus: Why are spiders good baseball players?
Cora: I have no clue.
Cyrus: Because they know how to catch flies.

* * *

Cyrus: Why did the driver throw money in the street?
Cora: I don't know.
Cyrus: So she could stop on a dime.

* * *

Cyrus: Why was the baby horse shivering?
Cora: Beats me.
Cyrus: He was a little "colt."

* * *

Cyrus: Why did the bee cross the road?
Cora: I can't guess.
Cyrus: To get to its honey.

* * *

Cyrus: Why did the grasshopper cross the lawn?
Cora: I have no idea.
Cyrus: Because he was a "grass-hopper."

* * *

Cyrus: Why did the otter cross the road?
Cora: You tell me.
Cyrus: To get to the "otter" side.

* * *

Cyrus: Why did the camper sneak silently into the tent?
Cora: I give up.
Cyrus: He didn't want to wake his sleeping bag.

* * *

Cyrus: Why is the moon like a dollar?
Cora: Who knows?
Cyrus: It has four quarters.

* * *

Cyrus: Why did the student eat his math test?
Cora: You've got me.
Cyrus: Because the teacher said it was a piece of cake.

* * *

Cyrus: Why did the whale eat two ships loaded with potatoes?
Cora: My mind is blank.
Cyrus: Because no one can eat just one potato ship.

Did Ya' Know?

Q: Only 17 percent of Americans can identify the man pictured on the U.S. $20 bill. Who is he?

A: Andrew Jackson.

* * *

Q: What is the smartest of all birds? (Hint: It's big and black).

A: The crow.

* * *

Q: Columbia, Yale, Princeton, and Harvard were the original Ivy League schools. Where did the name "Ivy League" come from?

A: From the Roman numeral IV for the four schools.

* * *

Q: How much weight does a baby whale gain each month during its first year of life?

A: About 2–3 tons.

* * *

More ice cream is sold on Sunday than on any other day.

Blendia & Bennet

Blendia: What is the whitest part of a baseball park?
Bennet: I have no clue.
Blendia: The bleachers.

* * *

Blendia: What does the hangman like to read?
Bennet: I don't know.
Blendia: The noosepaper.

* * *

Blendia: What are small black cats called in Tibet?
Bennet: Beats me.
Blendia: Kittens.

* * *

Blendia: What did the stamp say to the envelope?

Bennet: I can't guess.

Blendia: Stick with me, buddy, and we will go places together.

* * *

Blendia: What is the smallest bridge in the world?

Bennet: I have no idea.

Blendia: The bridge of your nose.

* * *

Blendia: What plays the piano and works for Chicken of the Sea?

Bennet: You tell me.

Blendia: Piano-tuna.

* * *

Blendia: What is long, likes water, and whistles "Dixie" backwards?

Bennet: I give up.

Blendia: General Robert E. Eel.

* * *

Blendia: What do they call a dinosaur that is always in a hurry?

Bennet: Who knows?

Blendia: A prontosaurus.

* * *

Blendia: What do they call a skeleton who will not get out of bed?

Bennet: You've got me.

Blendia: Lazy Bones.

* * *

Blendia: What would happen if an insane goat fell into a blender?

Bennet: My mind is blank.

Blendia: You would have a crazy, mixed-up kid.

Did Ya' Know?

A cubic mile of fog contains less than a gallon of water.

* * *

On average, a person spends about two years of his or her life on the phone.

* * *

More redheads are born in Scotland than in any other part of the world.

* * *

Rockets were first made by the Chinese more than 750 years ago.

* * *

A watermelon is actually a berry.

* * *

Q: What two popular cookie flavors originated in Mexico and were used by the Aztecs before Columbus visited the Americas in 1492?

A: Chocolate and vanilla.

I've Got an Answer

Jim: If you crossed a computer with an elephant, what would you have?

Jane: Search me.

Jim: A very big know-it-all.

* * *

Teacher: Why does lightning never strike in the same place twice?

Student: After lightning hits something, it's not the same place anymore.

* * *

Slim: Who was the famous Greek whom some think invented baseball?

Clem: I'm in the dark.

Slim: Homer.

* * *

Lisa: When someone asked the author how his business was doing, what did he say?

Christy: I pass.

Lisa: It's all write.

＊ ＊ ＊

Ruby: When a frog's car breaks down, what does he do?

Pearl: You've got me.

Ruby: He calls a toad truck.

＊ ＊ ＊

Q: When is a girl's dress like a frog?

A: When it's a jumper!

＊ ＊ ＊

Q: When is it safe to pet a lion?

A: When it's a dandelion.

＊ ＊ ＊

Q: When is the best time to jump on a trampoline?
A: Springtime!

* * *

Q: Who is Pizza's favorite relative?
A: Aunt Chovy.

* * *

Q: What does teacher rabbit read to her bunnies?
A: Hare-raising stories.

* * *

Q: Whom do birds marry?
A: Their tweethearts.

* * *

Q: If a carrot and a lettuce were to run a race, which one would win?
A: The lettuce because it's a head.

* * *

Q: If three lions were chasing you, what time would it be?

A: Three after one!

Did Ya' Know?

Q: What does the word *dinosaur* mean?
A: It comes from two Greek words meaning "terrible lizard."

* * *

Q: Where have dinosaur fossils been found?
A: On every continent on earth.

* * *

New York's Empire State Building was once struck by 500 lightning bolts in one year!

* * *

Cows can smell odors six miles away.

* * *

Q: According to research, what part of the human body will grow back after injury without scar tissue?

A: The tongue.

Tidbits

Piano tuner: I'm here to tune your piano.

Tami: I didn't call for a piano tuner.

Piano tuner: I know. Your neighbors did.

* * *

Owen: Was the lifeguard sincere about wearing sun block?

Cay: No, he was just going through the lotions.

* * *

Q: Does it take longer to run from first base to second, or from second base to third?

A: Second base to third, because there is a short stop between them.

* * *

Kati: My cat just had eight kittens.

Gabi: What do you call them?

Kati: Octo-pusses.

* * *

Jeff: Oh, Noel, before you leave...guess what I just bought?

Noel: What's that?

Jeff: A man came to the door and sold me the Nile River.

Noel: Egypt you (he gypped you).

* * *

Tony: My cat can talk.

Tina: No she can't.

Tony: Yes she can. I asked her what two minus two was, and she said nothing.

* * *

Dave: Does your dog bite?

Jane: No. Ginger snaps.

* * *

Stacy: I just found a horseshoe.

Sam: That's good luck.

Stacy: No it's not. It just means some poor horse is running around barefoot!

* * *

Gary: Your cough sounds a lot better.

Gina: Thanks, I've been practicing all night.

Did Ya' Know?

The *gluteus maximus,* or rump, is the strongest muscle in the human body.

* * *

Q: How often does the average American move to a new place during a lifetime?

A: Eleven times, or once every 6 years.

* * *

Astronauts aboard the space shuttle see 16 sunrises and sunsets a day.

* * *

About 6,000 languages are spoken in the world today.

* * *

Q: Each U.S. quarter has 119 grooves etched into its rim. How many grooves does a dime have?

A: 118.

Cordellia & Crosby

Cordellia: What do you get when you cross a turkey with a banjo?

Crosby: I have no clue.

Cordellia: A turkey who plucks himself!

* * *

Cordellia: What's a dog's favorite snack?

Crosby: I don't know.

Cordellia: Pup-corn.

* * *

Cordellia: What is the best way to raise a hippopotamus?

Crosby: Beats me.

Cordellia: With a crane.

* * *

Cordellia: What is green, has big eyes, and makes a loud noise?

Crosby: I can't guess.

Cordellia: A frog horn.

* * *

Cordellia: What is a wasp?

Crosby: I have no idea.

Cordellia: An insect that stings for its supper.

* * *

Cordellia: What did Tennessee?

Crosby: You tell me.

Cordellia: The same thing Arkansas.

* * *

Cordellia: What is served but never eaten?

Crosby: Who knows?

Cordellia: A volleyball.

* * *

Cordellia: What happens when you tell jokes about the stomach?

Crosby: You've got me.

Cordellia: You get belly laughs.

* * *

Cordellia: What can never be made right?

Crosby: My mind is blank.

Cordellia: Your left foot.

Did Ya' Know?

Q: What is the only metal that is liquid at room temperature?

A: Mercury.

* * *

The digestive tract (the tube that food passes through) in a person's body is about 30 feet long.

* * *

The average American eats eight pounds of pickles every year!

* * *

When an ostrich is in a hurry, it can cover a lot of ground. So how fast can these big steppers go? Nearly 45 miles per hour.

* * *

Dolphins can swim 37 miles per hour, while humans can swim only 5.19 miles per hour.

* * *

Q: Next to people, what mammals live longest?
A: Whales.

Gideon & Gloria

Gideon: What has three feet but can't walk?
Gloria: I can't guess.
Gideon: A yardstick!

* * *

Gideon: What school do soda jerks attend?
Gloria: You tell me.
Gideon: Sundae (Sunday) school!

* * *

Gideon: What tree is always unhappy?
Gloria: I give up.
Gideon: A blue spruce.

* * *

Gideon: What piece of wood is like a king?
Gloria: Who knows?
Gideon: A ruler.

* * *

Gideon: What did the leopard say in the cafeteria?
Gloria: My mind is blank.
Gideon: Save me a spot.

Did Ya' Know?

The average American eats 730 bologna sandwiches during his or her lifetime.

*   *   *

Q: How many teeth does a mosquito have?
A: 47.

*   *   *

Q: How much of the earth's surface is covered by clouds at any given time?
A: Two-thirds.

*   *   *

The average American spends one hour and 18 minutes every weekend doing laundry.

* * *

A beehive can hold up to 80,000 bees.

Who's There?

Knock, knock.
Who's there?
Gladys.
Gladys who?
Gladys see you.

* * *

Knock, knock.
Who's there?
Luke.
Luke who?
Luke who's there before you open the door.

* * *

Knock, knock.
Who's there?
Lyndon.
Lyndon who?
Lyndon me an ear, and I'll tell you another knock-knock joke.

* * *

Knock, knock.

Who's there?

Avenue.

Avenue who?

Avenue heard the good news? I've got more knock-knock jokes.

* * *

Knock, knock.

Who's there?

Heaven.

Heaven who?

Heaven seen you for a long, long time.

* * *

Knock, knock.

Who's there?

Thistle.

Thistle who?

Thistle not be the last time I knock on your door.

* * *

Knock, knock.
Who's there?
Lettuce.
Lettuce who?
Lettuce in and we'll tell you another knock-knock joke.

* * *

Knock, knock.
Who's there?
Carl.
Carl who?
Carl (car will) get you there faster than a bike.

* * *

Knock, knock.
Who's there?
Ewok.
Ewok who?
Ewocked the door—wet me in.

* * *

Knock, knock.
Who's there?
Stu.
Stu who?
Stu (it's too) late to hide!

* * *

Knock, knock.
Who's there?
Turnip.
Turnip who?
Turnip (turn up) the volume; I can't hear.

Did Ya' Know?

Q: What is the average life span of a cardinal (bird)?

A: 30 years.

* * *

Q: What U.S. president kept the most pets in the White House?

A: Teddy Roosevelt and his children kept cats, dogs, raccoons, a parrot, a pony, and even a bear. One daughter, Alice, named her snake Emily Spinach.

* * *

Your heart pumps the equivalent of about 4,200 gallons of blood every day.

* * *

Q: Who are some of the fastest swimmers in the sea?

A: Tuna and certain sharks are able to swim up to 50 miles per hour in short bursts.

* * *

Most people's legs are of slightly different lengths.

Lila & Lillian

Lila: What do you get when you cross a turtle with a porcupine?

Lillian: I have no clue.

Lila: A slowpoke!

* * *

Lila: What does Mickey Mouse's girlfriend drive?

Lillian: I don't know.

Lila: A Minnie van.

* * *

Lila: What's the most popular sport in Antarctica?

Lillian: Beats me.

Lila: South Polo.

* * *

Lila: What's a polar bear's favorite food?

Lillian: I can't guess.

Lila: Ice Krispies.

* * *

Lila: What did one firecracker say to the other?

Lillian: I give up.

Lila: My pop's bigger than your pop!

* * *

Lila: What runs around all day and lies on the floor all night with its tongue hanging out?

Lillian: Who knows?

Lila: A shoe.

* * *

Lila: What subject do you study at the mall?

Lillian: You've got me.

Lila: Buyology.

Did Ya' Know?

Q: What do the three colors in the U.S. flag represent?

A: Red—courage
White—purity
Blue—justice

* * *

Air Force One, the jet that transports the president of the United States, has a conference room that can convert into an operating room!

* * *

While getting dressed, 58 percent of Americans put their right leg into their pants first.

* * *

There are 193 different kinds of apes and monkeys in the world.

* * *

Q: What is the hardest natural substance on earth?
A: A diamond.

* * *

Q: How much action do your eyeballs see each year?
A: In the course of a year, your eyes move up, down, and sideways about 36,000,000 times and you blink about 84,000,000 times.

Clyde & Colby

Clyde: What do people sing during their baths?
Colby: I have no clue.
Clyde: Soap operas.

* * *

Clyde: What runs all over town but never comes inside?
Colby: You tell me.
Clyde: The street.

* * *

Clyde: What happened when Garfield explored the freezer?
Colby: I give up.
Clyde: Curiosity chilled the cat.

* * *

Clyde: What is the saddest tree?
Colby: Who knows?
Clyde: The weeping willow.

* * *

Clyde: What is a clown's favorite snack?
Colby: You've got me.
Clyde: Peanut riddle.

* * *

Clyde: What does a bee wear when it dresses up?
Colby: My mind is blank.
Clyde: A yellow jacket.

Did Ya' Know?

Q: Which shark has the most teeth?

A: The peaceful, easygoing whale shark has more than 7,000 teeth.

* * *

Most electric eels release an electric charge of about 350 volts (about five times more electricity than an average light bulb). The most powerful electric eel can produce a shock of 650 volts.

* * *

When you run, the pounding taken by your feet is equivalent to three to four times your body weight.

* * *

Q: In what ancient civilization was a red flag a signal for battle?

A: Roman.

* * *

Q: In what country is red used as a holiday and wedding color for good luck?

A: China.

* * *

Muscles make up 40 percent of a person's total body weight.

Wanda & Wilson

Wanda: What's black and white and red all over?

Wilson: I have no clue.

Wanda: An embarrassed penguin!

* * *

Wanda: What does Saturn like to read?

Wilson: I don't know.

Wanda: Comet books.

* * *

Wanda: What do you get when you cross a mummy with a CD?

Wilson: Beats me.

Wanda: A wrap song!

* * *

Wanda: What did the buffalo say to his son when he left on vacation?

Wilson: I can't guess.

Wanda: Bison! (Bye son!)

* * *

Wanda: What do you get when you milk a nervous cow?

Wilson: I have no idea.

Wanda: A milk shake.

* * *

Wanda: What did the caveman eat for lunch?

Wilson: You tell me.

Wanda: Club sandwiches.

* * *

Wanda: What bird can lift a building?

Wilson: I give up.

Wanda: A crane.

* * *

Wanda: What country can be served on dinner tables?

Wilson: Who knows?

Wanda: Turkey.

* * *

Wanda: What does an acrobat do when he reads a schoolbook?

Wilson: You've got me.

Wanda: He flips through the pages.

* * *

Wanda: What did the bald man say when he got a comb as a gift?

Wilson: My mind is blank.

Wanda: Thanks very much—I'll never part with it!

Did Ya' Know?

Q: In what country is red a color for mourning?
A: South Africa.

* * *

A baseball hit by a bat can travel as fast as 120 miles per hour!

* * *

Medieval Europeans believed that gingerbread cookies made in the shape of hearts could ward off evil.

* * *

Forty percent of the world's annual almond crop is sold to chocolate makers.

＊ ＊ ＊

Q: How many eyes does the horseshoe crab have?
A: Ten.

Carter & Casey

Carter: Why did they let the turkey play in the band?

Casey: I have no clue.

Carter: Because it had drumsticks.

* * *

Carter: Why are horses bad dancers?

Casey: I don't know.

Carter: Because they have two left feet.

* * *

Carter: Why can you always bet on another wave rolling in?

Casey: Beats me.

Carter: Because it's a shore thing.

* * *

Carter: Why did the chicken cross the playground?

Casey: I have no idea.

Carter: To get to the other slide.

* * *

Carter: Why did the kids wear bathing suits to school?

Casey: You tell me.

Carter: Because they rode in a carpool.

* * *

Carter: Why do watermelons have weddings?

Casey: Who knows?

Carter: Because they cantaloupe.

* * *

Carter: Why did the little boy put hay in his bed?

Casey: You've got me.

Carter: To feed his nightmare.

* * *

Carter: Why don't blind people skydive?

Casey: My mind is blank.

Carter: Because it scares their seeing-eye dogs.

* * *

Carter: Why do most cars cry?

Casey: That's a mystery.

Carter: Because they have windshield weepers.

Did Ya' Know?

Q: In ancient times, what was given to the first-prize winners in the Olympics?

A: A stalk of celery.

* * *

Q: All the planets in the solar system are named after Roman gods except which one?

A: Earth.

* * *

Q: Nearly three-quarters of all land animals and plants live where?

A: In forests.

* * *

At night, a cat can see about six times better than a human.

* * *

Q: Which is bigger: Maine or Switzerland?
A: Maine.

* * *

The world's heaviest mammal, the blue whale, weighs up to 40 million times more than the lightest bumble-bee. A blue whale can grow up to 100 feet long and can weigh 150 tons. That's equal to 20 elephants.

Other Books by Bob Phillips

The All-New Clean Joke Book

*Awesome Book
of Heavenly Humor*

*Awesome Dinosaur Jokes
for Kids*

*Awesome Good Clean Jokes
for Kids*

*The Best of the Good
Clean Jokes*

*Bob Phillips' Encyclopedia
of Good Clean Jokes*

*Controlling Your Emotions
Before They Control You*

Dude, Got Another Joke?

*Extremely Good Clean
Jokes for Kids*

How Can I Be Sure?

Over the Hill & On a Roll

*Over the Next Hill
& Still Rolling*

Personal Prayer List

*So You Want to Be
a Bible Trivia Expert?*

*Super Cool Jokes
and Games for Kids*

*Super-Duper Good
Clean Jokes for Kids*

*A Tackle Box
of Fishing Funnies*

*Totally Cool Clean
Jokes for Kids*

*The World's Greatest
Collection of Clean Jokes*

*The World's Greatest
Collection of Knock-Knock
Jokes for Kids*

For information send a self-addressed stamped
envelope to:

Family Services
P.O. Box 9363
Fresno, California 93702

Other Books by Steve Russo

The Seduction of Our Children

The Devil's Playground

Halloween: What's a Christian to Do?

Keeping Christ in Christmas

Why Celebrate Easter?

Wild and Wooly Clean Jokes

Squeaky Clean Jokes for Kids

For information send a self-addressed stamped envelope to:

Steve Russo
P.O. Box 1549
Ontario, California 91762
www.steverusso.com